# Women
## of the
# Wild West

# WOMEN *of the* WILD WEST

## *Biographies from many cultures*

### *by RUTH PELZ*

**OPEN HAND**
PUBLISHING, LLC

OPEN HAND PUBLISHING, LLC
Greensboro, North Carolina
www.openhand.com

**OPEN HAND PUBLISHING, LLC**
P.O. Box 20207
Greensboro, NC 27420
336-292-8585 / 336-292-8588 FAX
info@openhand.com
www.openhand.com

**OPEN HAND**
PUBLISHING, LLC

Book design by David Serra
Cover by Deb Figen
Cover photo by Edward S. Curtis

**Library of Congress Cataloging-in-Publication Data**
Pelz, Ruth.
    Women of the Wild West : biographies from many cultures / by Ruth Pelz. — 1st ed.
        p.    cm.
    Includes bibliographical references.
    ISBN 0-940880-49-0 (clothcover) : $12.95 -- ISBN 0-940880-50-4 (paperback) : $6.95
        1. Women pioneers—West (U.S.)—Biography—Juvenile literature.
2.  Women—West (U.S.)—Biography—Juvenile literature.   3.  West (U.S.)—Biography—Juvenile literature.    I.  Title.
    F596.P45   1994
    920.72'0978—dc20
                                                    94-1031
                                                    CIP


**Second Printing 2003**
Printed in the United States of America
07  06  05  04  03      6  5  4  3  2

# ACKNOWLEDGMENTS

In the history books I read as a child, women rarely appeared, and, seeing no one who looked much like me in those books, I soon lost interest.

Even if my teachers had thought to correct this problem, they would have had a hard time doing so. For the stories of women in our nation's past, no matter how extraordinary, were rarely recorded.

Fortunately, a lot has changed since then. In the last few decades, many dedicated scholars have done the hard work of sifting through mountains of historical records to piece together the names and lives of women who were there and who played important roles.

It is because of their efforts that this book is possible. Several of those scholars' names appear in the brief bibliography included at the end of the book. In particular, I would like to acknowledge Ruthanne Lum McCunn, who has researched and written about the first generation of Asian American women, including Mary Bong and many others; William Loren Katz, whose research on *The Black West* inspired this book and others in this series; the wonderfully helpful staff of the University of Washington Libraries, Special Collections Division; and my original publisher, Anna Johnson, who gave an enormous amount of time and effort to ensure that these stories, and others like them, are told. Thanks, finally, to Open Hand's current publisher, Richard Koritz, for seeing the value of this book and keeping it in circulation.

*~ RUTH PELZ*

# Table of Contents

# Sacajawea

*Born: 1786 • Died: 1812*

The first men and women in the American West were the people we now call Indians or Native Americans. They lived here for thousands of years before any other people came.

Each Indian group or tribe had a somewhat different way of life. Women from two tribes are included in this book, the Shoshone and the Paiute.

The first U.S. citizens to cross the western lands were led by Merriwether Lewis and William Clark. One woman traveled with these explorers. She was a Shoshone Indian named **Sacajawea**.

Sacajawea's husband was a French Canadian fur trader who spoke several Indian languages. Lewis and Clark hired him to be their translator. Sacajawea and her baby traveled with him and proved very helpful to the expedition. She is one of the earliest Native American women whose story was written down.

*I*t all happened in an instant. A sudden, powerful gust of wind struck the boat. The sail whipped around wildly. The boat appeared to leap sideways and then tilted dangerously toward shore. Foaming water rushed in over the sides. The crew members panicked. The boatman was totally out of control. A few more minutes and all was lost!

From the river bank, the explorers Lewis and Clark watched in horror. In that boat were books, medicines, tools, and supplies — everything necessary for the success of their journey. Without these, a year of work would be wasted.

Then one man's voice rose above the screams. "Oars! Get to your oars! Pull hard. Get the buckets and bail out this water!" The crew did as they were told.

Shoshone woman.

While others paid attention to the boat, one person remembered the supplies. She was the one woman on board. Her name was Sacajawea. Quickly and purposefully, she leaned into the churning water and grabbed the bundles that had washed overboard.

The explorers breathed a grateful sigh of relief. The journey was saved! Their supplies were secure.

Lewis and Clark and their party went on to complete one of the most important explorations in American history. It was the first trip across North America, from the Mississippi River to the Pacific Ocean. It took two years. Sacajawea, a member of the Shoshone tribe, was the only woman to make the trip.

Saving the bundles was not the first thing she had done to help the explorers. It would not be the last.

Sacajawea knew several Native languages. She was able to communicate with many of the people the explorers met. She shared valuable knowledge of Native cultures. She helped the explorers find food. She told them about the places she knew. But her most important contribution would come later.

It was several months after the storm struck the boat. The explorers had traveled high into the Rocky Mountains. These lands of steep cliffs and green valleys were Sacajawea's home.

It was here, as a child, that she learned which plants were good to eat. She learned to make pots and baskets and to fill them with tasty roots, nuts, and berries.

Like other Shoshone girls, Sacajawea could make soft leather clothing from animal skins. She could start a fire in less than a minute by rolling a stick in dry grasses.

The Shoshones' life was not easy. Plants and animals were scarce in these mountains. Many times, the hunters returned to camp empty-handed. Then there was nothing to eat but cakes of dried berries.

There were many days of hunger. But there were good times, too. There were times of games and play. There were days of dancing. All year long, Sacajawea looked forward to the dances of late winter. Everyone took part—men, women, boys and girls. But for her, those winters came to an early end.

She was less than fourteen years old when the Shoshones were attacked by another tribe. It was frightening! Galloping horses thundered through the camp. Arrows whizzed by. Children were crying. All was confusion. Sacajawea ran and ran but could not escape. She was captured!

Days of travel followed. The strangers took her farther and farther from her family and the beautiful valleys that were her home. The long trip ended in a Native village near the Missouri River. It was there that Sacajawea met her husband, a French Canadian fur trader named Toussaint. It was there that her first baby was born.

That same winter of the baby's birth, Lewis and Clark came to the village. They spent the winter with the tribe.

The explorers knew they would need interpreters who could speak Native languages. They hired Toussaint for the job. Sacajawea accompanied them, carrying her baby on the long, long journey.

Imagine this. Many western Native American tribes had never seen a white person. They certainly had not seen a large group of white travelers, like the one that accompanied Lewis and Clark. So many strange-looking people in strange clothing, speaking a language that Native people could not understand! It may have been very frightening. But seeing

Sacajawea and other members of the Lewis and Clark expedition.

Sacajawea and her baby, people were less afraid. The two of them made it easier for the explorers to meet and communicate with the tribes.

Each day of travel brought Sacajawea closer to her Shoshone home. By summer, they reached lands that she remembered. "Here," she said one day. "This is where the fighting took place. This is where I was captured."

Over the next weeks, Sacajawea pointed out a way across the Rocky Mountains. She told where the Shoshones camped in summer.

This was important information. The explorers had traveled a long way in their boats, but here the rivers were too swift and rocky. A boat could not be used. To finish their journey, the travelers would need horses.

The Shoshones were famous for the horses they raised.

The explorers had brought beads, tools, blankets, and other things to trade for horses. Now they had to find the Shoshones and convince them to make an exchange. The success of the trip depended on it.

In August the meeting finally happened. For Sacajawea, it was the most wonderful day of the trip. She was walking along when she saw a group of people approaching. As the people drew closer, Sacajawea began to dance and leap for joy. They were Shoshones! She had found her friends and family at last!

That afternoon, Lewis and Clark called Sacajawea to help them. "We will meet with the chief now and talk about buying the horses. Come and translate for us."

What a happy surprise! The chief was her own brother, Cameahwait. She threw her arms around him. There were tears in her eyes.

With Sacajawea's help, the bargain was made. The explorers got the horses they needed. The journey continued.

Sacajawea accompanied the explorers all the way to the Pacific Ocean and back again, to the city of Saint Louis, Missouri. However, city life didn't suit Toussaint and Sacajawea. They longed for the quiet of the Native villages. They returned to the frontier.

A few years after returning, Sacajawea died. She was only about twenty-six years old. But in that short lifetime, she earned her place in American history.

# Juana Briones de Miranda

*Born: 1796 • Died: 1899*

The first foreign visitors to the American West came from Spain. Texas, California, and other south-western states were once Spanish land. Santa Fe, New Mexico is the oldest city in the West. It was settled by the Spanish more than three hundred years ago.

Some women in Spanish America became wealthy landowners and important community leaders. **Juana Briones de Miranda** was one of them.

"*P*edro. Pedroooo! Where is that lazy helper when I need him?" The children heard their mother calling.

"Listen," said *Manuela*, the oldest. "It must be time to milk the cows. Let's go watch."

The children scampered through the family fruit orchard to the edge of the corral. Inside the fence were a dozen wild-eyed cows and their calves. They were lean, scruffy, angry-looking beasts. The cows had long, pointed horns as sharp as knives.

The first Spanish settlers in the American Southwest were Catholic missionaries. This is one of their missions.

Milking one of those California cattle was a challenge, and the children knew it. That's why they had come.

Soon, Pedro arrived, a long rope called a *reata* in one hand. Calmly, he unfastened the corral gate and went inside. The children watched expectantly.

In one swift, smooth movement, Pedro tossed a rope over a cow's head. She bellowed, stomped, and tossed her horns. But Pedro dragged her out of the corral. He tied the rope securely to a sturdy tree trunk. He tied the animal's back legs to the tree also. Then he grinned and sat down for a rest. Not for long, however.

The children's mother had arrived. She carried a bucket in one hand and a stool in the other. "Ay Pedro!" she screamed. "What are you doing sitting down? There's plenty more work to be done!"

*Señora* Juana Briones de Miranda was a hard worker herself, and she expected the same of her servants. It seemed to the children that she was always doing three things at once.

Now, she sat down on her stool and began to milk the struggling cow. She barked out orders to Pedro and conversed with the children at the same time. She calmed the angry cow and planned the day's work on the ranch.

In those days, when California was part of Mexico, ranching was the main business, and Juana had always been part of it. As a child, she had watched the *vaqueros* at work and dreamed one day of having a ranch of her own.

The yearly cattle round-ups, or *rodeos*, were the best time of year. How well she remembered them!

At *rodeo* time, Juana and her twin sister Maria woke early. They were too excited to sleep. They knew that when the work was over, the *fiesta* would begin.

Everyone came. There was singing and dancing long into the night. There was a big barbecue and plenty of good food to eat. There were contests of cowboy skills. The party went on for days.

Ranching life must be the best life there is, thought Juana. She grew up learning everything about it she could. Later, that knowledge would serve her well.

At the age of twenty-four, Juana married Apolinario Miranda, a corporal in the Mexican army. They settled near the *presidio*, or army post, by San Francisco Bay. They had eight children.

Spanish-speaking ranchers, or *rancheros*, celebrated special occasions with music and dance.

But the marriage was not a happy one. Corporal Miranda kept getting drunk and in trouble. Finally, he disappeared, leaving Juana to care for the children and their land alone.

She managed unusually well. Each year, her cattle ranch produced plenty of tallow and hides. The tallow, cooked down from animal fat, would be sold to make soap and candles. The dried cattle hides could be traded for flour and cloth and other items the ships brought in. In fact, hides were such

View down Stockton Street in early San Francisco.

important trade items that they were sometimes called "California dollars."

Juana also raised fruits and vegetables. She sold milk from her cows. She climbed into the hills and harvested wild mint, *Yerba Buena*. She used it to make a delicious tea.

Visitors to the Briones' adobe home looked forward to that sweet tea and to good conversation. But visitors were few. Life was lonely by the bay. There were soldiers and priests and Indians in the area. But there were few other families like hers nearby. Juana missed the picnics and barbecues, the wonderful music and dances she had known as a child.

One day, there was wonderful news. A family had settled down by the bay, in a quiet cove. They hoped to start a village, a *pueblo*. Happy for neighbors at last, Juana decided to move.

*11*

She built a new adobe house near the bay.

Juana Briones was one of the very first settlers of that village. The settlers called it *Yerba Buena*, after the wild mint. But today it is the city of San Francisco.

*Señora* Briones was a well-known member of that growing community. She cared for the sick and needy. She helped deliver babies. Many people were cured by her simple medicines and inspired by her energy. She was famous for her hospitality, too.

But Juana still missed the ranching life. When she was nearly fifty, she realized her dream. She bought a large *rancho* south of town. She managed it well and lived there until she was very old.

## Pronunciation Guide

| | |
|---|---|
| Juana | WHAH-nah |
| Manuela | mahn-WELL-ah |
| reata | ray-AH-tah |
| señora | sen-YOR-ah |
| vaquero | vah-KAIR-oh |
| rodeo | roh-DAY-oh |
| fiesta | fee-ESS-tah |
| presidio | preh-SID-ee-oh |
| ranchero | rahn-CHAIR-oh |
| Yerba Buena | YAIR-bah BWAY-na |
| pueblo | PWEB-loh |
| rancho | RAHN-cho |

# Biddy Mason

*Born: about 1820 • Died: 1891*

Early visitors to the West returned with wonderful stories. They told of vast lands, freedom, and great opportunities.

The trip west was not easy then. There were no roads across the land and no bridges across the rivers. The only way to get there was to walk, ride a horse, or travel in a covered wagon. There were plenty of dangers and few comforts along the way.

Still, thousands of families decided to go. They packed their belongings into small, wooden wagons, pulled by oxen. Cattle and horses followed behind. The path they made became known as the Oregon Trail. Among the travelers were a few African Americans. Some were slaves, accompanying their owners. Others were free blacks, in search of freedom and a better life. **Biddy Mason** was one of the African American women who made the trip.

"*M*ama, I'm tired," said the little girl. "It's hot and I'm tired of walking. Why can't we stop now? Why can't we stay where we are?"

"Hush now," said Biddy, comforting her daughter. "I know you're tired. I've had more than enough of traveling myself. But it isn't my choice, child. It's Mr. Robert Smith says if we're walking or staying. And Mr. Smith is a traveling kind of man. You get up in the wagon with your sister for a while."

Sometimes it seemed they would never stop traveling. First there had been the long trip to Utah. All day Biddy had walked along behind the wagons, tending the cattle. For months they walked, getting farther and farther from Mississippi. It was a hard trip, especially for the children. But what could Biddy do? She was born a slave. She was a slave today. Her master told her to walk across the plains and she did it.

They had been in Utah for only one year when word came of a new settlement in Southern California. The master, Robert Smith, decided to go. Again the wagons were packed. Again they began the long days of walking.

Biddy had plenty of time for thinking along the way. What she mostly thought about was freedom. As a child she had never known an African American person who wasn't a slave. Oh, she heard about them, about the ones who escaped to the North. But it was all so hard to imagine!

Then came the trip west. Things were different here. She had seen African American families, traveling west with their own wagons! Just think of it! They planned to find their own

A wagon train.

land, start their own farms, or find work in the towns. Biddy kept thinking about them.

Then there was Salt Lake City. Mormon families had come there from all over the country. Some came from the South and brought slaves with them. Many families came from the northern states, though, where slavery wasn't allowed. It was different, all right. It got you thinking.

Biddy looked down at her bare feet. They were tired and sore and covered with dust. These feet walked every mile from Mississippi, she thought. And they remember every step. They have walked for Mr. Smith and his family. They have walked after his crops and his wagons and his cattle. But some-day they are going to walk for me. Someday these feet will walk me to freedom! I'm sure of it.

A few days later, the tired travelers arrived at San Bernardino, California. It was a lovely place. It was their new home.

There were many reasons to enjoy living in California in 1852. The climate was pleasant. The land was good. The air was fresh and warm. Cities were booming. Everywhere there was a sense of promise and excitement.

The most important thing for Biddy was the promise of freedom. She had heard people talking. The new state of California did not permit slavery, they said. By law all people here were free. Biddy looked again at her dusty traveling feet. Soon, she said to herself, soon.

Three years passed. Life was pretty good, but Mr. Smith must have loved traveling. Even this beautiful settlement could not hold him. He decided to move again, this time to Texas. The wagons were loaded and made ready to go.

Biddy knew she had to act. As soon as the wagons left San Bernardino, she began looking for an opportunity. She found one. Somehow she sent word to the sheriff in Los Angeles. He stopped the wagons before they left California.

"I hear you have slaves in your party," said the sheriff. "I suppose you know that's against the law. Is it true?"

Biddy came forward. In all her life this was the first time she had ever spoken to a white sheriff. Still her voice was strong. "It is true," she said. "Mr. Smith is taking us to Texas and we don't want to go."

That statement led to the most important slavery trial in Southern California. Biddy and another slave woman and their

Biddy Mason.

children were taken to court. Biddy spoke to the judge, and once again, her words were strong and clear: "I want to stay in California. I want to be free."

The judge sided with Biddy. He scolded Mr. Smith for

breaking the law. He gave all the slaves their freedom.

Biddy gathered up her children and said, "We are moving once more, but it won't be very far. We are going to Los Angeles, and this time," she said, looking at her tired feet, "I am walking for me!"

She started her new life by taking Biddy Mason as her full name. She went to work as a nurse and housekeeper. Before long she saved enough money to buy a house. Soon she bought other property too. Biddy Mason was a good businesswoman. She became one of the wealthiest African Americans in Los Angeles.

She shared that wealth with others. She gave land to build schools and hospitals and nursing homes. She supported the education of African American children and helped people in need. Biddy Mason had come a long way from that slave's cabin in Mississippi. She still remembered the walking. And she made sure she helped others along their way.

# Mother Joseph (Esther Pariseau)

*Born: 1823  •  Died: 1902*

Even before pioneers crossed the Oregon Trail, a few brave women journeyed westward. They were missionaries. They went west to teach Native Americans about the Christian religion and way of life. **Mother Joseph** was one of the best-known.

"*N*ow, Mama?" asked Esther. "Now may I go? I finished my sewing."

Madame Pariseau sighed. "*Oui*," she said. "You may go. But don't be late for supper."

Esther Pariseau stepped out of the stone farmhouse. Smiling, she hurried to the carriage shop where her father was working.

Esther could spin, weave, sew, cook, and garden as well as her sisters. (Well, almost!) But her father's work was so much more exciting! Monsieur Pariseau was a carriage-maker, one of the best in all Quebec. Esther loved to watch him work.

Often, he let her help. She sanded the wooden carriage parts until they were smooth as glass. Then she oiled and polished them until they gleamed.

She learned which trees gave strong, tough wood for the body of the carriage. She learned how to cut the wood and fit the pieces together. Every week, it seemed, she learned something more.

Today she was especially eager to get to the shop. She was making her mother a wooden sewing box. It was almost finished.

"Papa," Esther called. "Come and see mother's gift." Her father put down his tools and came to look.

"You've done a good job," he said. "You have many talents, Esther. I hope you have many chances to use them."

The truth was, there were few opportunities for a girl like Esther Pariseau. In fact, she thought, there was really only one. "I want to be a nun," she decided. "I want to go west."

Her family supported the decision. Esther joined the group of nuns called the Sisters of Providence. A few years later, she set out on her great adventure!

Together with four other nuns, she traveled to the northwest corner of the United States. Esther was chosen to be their leader. She received a new name to go with the responsibility. She would be called Mother Joseph.

The town of Vancouver, Washington, was home to many pioneer families. It had a church and a military fort. But there was no house for the nuns. All five would have to sleep in a single, small room.

Mother Joseph of the Sacred Heart, c. 1900.

Fort Vancouver, Washington, from an 1854 print by Gustavus Sohon.

Mother Joseph looked at that room and went to work. Out came her carpentry tools. She began cutting wood. She made bunks and a table. Boxes served as chairs. The sisters had a home.

There was much to do in that little pioneer community. The Sisters of Providence started an orphanage. They taught school. They tended the sick. But they needed a hospital.

Mother Joseph decided to build one. That first hospital was little more than a cabin. It was the size of a schoolroom and had just four beds. It was filled with patients before it was even finished, but it would have to do.

The town needed an orphanage too. The army commander at Fort Vancouver donated the lumber. Mother Joseph supervised the construction. The orphanage was built.

Pioneer family in the Pacific Northwest.

In her lifetime, Mother Joseph founded eleven hospitals, two orphanages, and seven schools. Some are still standing.

All of that building cost money, and Mother Joseph set out to raise it. She mounted a horse and rode off through the wilderness. She followed long and lonely trails to remote communities.

"Won't you help us take care of the children and the sick?" she asked the families she met. People helped, even if they had only a little money themselves.

Those trips could be dangerous. One or two women, traveling alone, carrying money, were targets for wandering thieves. Mother Joseph ran into them more than once, but she was never afraid. And she never lost her money.

She kept right on working, traveling, and building until she was nearly eighty years old. Few people in the Northwest could match Mother Joseph's accomplishments.

In honor of those accomplishments, the Washington State government paid her a great honor. They chose her to be one of only two Washington State citizens whose statue is in the United States Capitol building.

# Mary Bong

*Born: 1879 • Died: 1958*

A few years after the Oregon Trail was opened, there was exciting news. Gold was discovered in California! People from many countries came to the American West, hoping to get rich.

Among them were thousands of Chinese men and a few Chinese women. One of these was **Mary Bong**. Like other women who lived on the western frontier, she faced a life of hard work and many challenges.

"*G*old! They've found gold in California!" The news spread faster than a squirrel can skitter up a tree.

Even far across the ocean, in the busy port cities of China, people could talk of little else. "*Gum Shan*," they said excitedly. "There's a mountain of gold in America. Anyone can go there and become rich."

Dreams of American gold gave hope to China's poorest residents for many years. Among the dreamers was a bold,

Chinese names were difficult for other Americans to pronounce. Many of the women were called "China Mary." Like Mary Bong, this woman's original Chinese name is unknown.

young girl, just ten years old. "One day," she said, "I too will go to *Gum Shan*."

"Silly girl," some people laughed. "It's hard enough for a grown man to buy a ticket to America. How will you ever have enough money for the trip?"

But she was determined. Hadn't the dream of a better life already made her run away from home and come to this city? Wasn't she already working as hard as a person twice her age and earning her own pay? Each week she set aside a few precious coins, and the pile was growing. She knew her dream would come true.

It did. She bought her ticket, and at age fifteen she was on a ship, crossing the Pacific Ocean. The year was 1895.

Perhaps it was there on the ship that she received her new name, Mary. This brave girl's Chinese name is no longer known.

By then, many years had passed since gold was discovered in California. America was still a land of wealth and opportunities, but few of those opportunities were open to the Chinese. They were not allowed to own land in America. They could not find good jobs.

For many years, Chinese people were not even allowed to enter the United States. Mary was not discouraged, though. She bought a ticket to Canada instead.

The ocean trip was long and uncomfortable. The sleeping areas were crowded and stuffy. The ship rolled and tossed on the waves, making many passengers sick. Mary managed better than most. She was used to life on the water.

As a young child, she had lived on a boat with her family. That was common in southeastern China. Hard times had come, though, and the family had to go on land to work on farms. Even young children worked from sunrise to sunset every day. They picked and planted, stooped and carried, until every muscle in their bodies was sore. Mary ran away from that life. Ahead of her lay a new life, exciting and unknown.

What a day that was when they first saw North America! Mary hurried to the deck to look. Ahead of her were tall, snow-covered mountains, the tallest she had ever seen.

Everything seems so big here, she thought. Will there be a place for a girl like me?

The ship docked in Vancouver, a growing town near the foot of the mountains. Mary was happy to reach the bustling neighborhood known as Chinatown. Here were people speaking her language. The familiar sights and smells reminded her of home.

In a short time, Mary met and married a Chinese businessman named Ah Bong. They moved to Sitka, Alaska, where Ah Bong owned a restaurant.

In those days, Sitka was a rough little frontier village, with only a few buildings. Mary ran the restaurant. She served up simple meals to the miners and settlers in town.

Then, Ah Bong died, and Mary had some hard years, caring for her two children alone.

In time, she remarried. Her second husband was an energetic Scandinavian named Fred Johnson.

Sitka was a small pioneer town when Mary Bong arrived. She was the first Chinese woman to live there.

Mary's years of hard work didn't end with marriage. Like every woman living on the American frontier, she had to work long hours just to get by.

The extraordinary life of Mary Bong included just about every kind of work the frontier offered. The first work she and Fred tried was mining. Mary learned how to blast a tunnel through the rock, how to run the mine. She spent her days underground with her husband, shoveling ore.

Finally they saved enough money to buy land. They decided to start a dairy. Fred and Mary had to chop down trees, clear the land, and put up buildings. The dairy didn't work out, though, and the Johnsons sold it. They decided to try something new.

Young members of Tlingit tribe in Sitka, where Mary Bong lived.

Next, Mary and Fred set out into the wilderness to look for gold and furs. They scooped up panfuls of gravel along river shores, hoping to find nuggets of gold. They set traps in icy waters to catch animals with soft and valuable furs.

But that was a harsh and lonely life, with few rewards. Mary and Fred soon tired of it and turned to yet another job, fishing. Mary, who had run away from life on the water so long ago, was back on the water again.

She was the only woman running a salmon boat then. She was good at it. Mary went out alone, even in thick fog and bad weather. She was braver, they said, than most of the men. "You can't run for shelter every time it gets rough," said Mary.

That was Mary. She never ran from hard work or rough times. She used every bit of her great strength and determination to survive.

# May Arkwright Hutton

*Born: 1860 • Died: 1915*

At the end of the trail, the pioneer women had much work to do. At first, they had to make nearly everything their families needed. They wove cloth and sewed clothing. They farmed and cooked and stored food for winter. They made candles and soap and shoes and mattresses.

As more people arrived, towns grew up. Western women had more opportunities. They found work as teachers and shopkeepers, as well as farmers and ranchers.

After the railroads were built, the trip west became much easier. More and more women joined the westward movement. **May Arkwright Hutton** was one of the independent women who came west alone, started a business, and became quite successful.

*M*ay Arkwright clung tightly to her grandfather's hand. She looked up at the noisy crowd of adults that surrounded them. "What's happening?" she asked.

"I'll lift you up, child, so you can see," he replied.

May looked. In the center of the crowd, a young man stood on an old wooden box. He spoke forcefully.

"It's a crime," he said. "We work hard all day long and can't earn enough for a decent life. Our children go to bed hungry. There's only one solution. Working people must join together. We must fight for change."

May knew that Grandfather would discuss the speech with his friends later on. They would talk about the problems of the nation and how they might be solved. And May would listen. Often, she fell asleep in grandfather's soothing arms as the men talked on and on.

May Arkwright grew up with many dreams. Dreams of helping others. Dreams of adventure. Dreams of a life free of poverty and want.

She was waiting and watching for opportunities. Like many young people of her time, she felt certain those opportunities were in the West.

An advertisement from the railroad caught her eye. "Come to Idaho," it said. "There's gold in the Rocky Mountains."

May knew just what she would do. "Where there is gold, there are hungry miners with money to spend," she said. "I'm going to start a restaurant."

At age twenty-three, she arrived in Idaho with just one

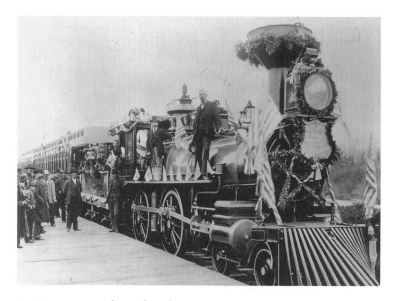

Coming west on the railroad.

basket of clothes. Before long, she opened her restaurant in a two-room shack. She set up a big table in the front room and began serving meals.

May Arkwright was a good cook. And no one, it appeared, enjoyed her cooking more than she. May was a big woman, tall and heavy. Her personality matched her size. May said what was on her mind and didn't care who heard. She worked hard for what she wanted and what she believed was right.

The little restaurant soon was filled with miners and railroad men. One of the customers was a quiet railroad engineer named Al Hutton. He and May decided to get married.

The Huttons bought a small house in Wallace, Idaho, near the big Bunker Hill mine. It didn't take May long to learn

Children of a western mining community.

about the problems of the miners.

"Listen," she told Al. "Those miners work underground from dawn to dark. Many days, they never see the sun at all. And their work is dangerous. There are deadly accidents every year. I swear, the mine owners treat their horses better than they treat those men. We've got to do something!"

May joined the efforts to help the miners start a union. Many early meetings were held in the Huttons' home.

Meanwhile, May and Al kept working. They saved some money and decided to invest in a mine themselves. With a small group of partners, they bought some land. Then they started digging, drilling, blasting, and hauling out rock. They went to the mine on weekends or after work, whenever they had time. Men and women all did their share. The work went

May (sitting), and Al (with kitten), and their partners at the Hercules Mine, Burke, Idaho, 1901.

on for nearly eight years.

Some of the partners grew discouraged, but not May. "Don't quit now," she urged them. "This mine will make us rich one day. I know it will."

That day finally came. Deep in the mine, the partners found the richest ore that anyone had seen. It was loaded with lead and silver! May and Al and the others all became millionaires.

May said, "The Lord gave me money to serve." And she did. She helped children and workers and people in need. Most of all, she worked to win women the right to vote. She wrote letters, gave speeches, organized meetings, and

Women working for the right to vote.

talked to government leaders. She met with lawmakers, lawyers, governors, and even presidents. Working with other men and women around the Northwest, she achieved her goal.

Whatever May was doing, people knew about it. She was never retiring or shy. Not everyone liked her, but no one could overlook her. She was a big woman in every sense of the word.

# Kate Chapman

*Born: 1870 • Died: ?*

One of the ways we know about the lives of women in the Old West is through their writings. **Kate Chapman** was an African American writer who grew up in the pioneer town of Yankton in Dakota Territory. She wrote about the life in her town and the accomplishments of other African Americans.

*Y*oung Kate Chapman lay on her bed and listened to the steamboat whistle. How she loved that sound! It seemed to tell all the stories that the river knew.

Kate sighed. She had been sick for such a long time now! One disease had followed another. She could hardly remember the last time she walked beside the river herself.

But the sound of the steamboats opened the doors of her imagination. Kate closed her eyes. She could picture the scene that must be taking place at the docks.

She imagined the big white boat, tied up with ropes as thick

Kate Chapman.

as her waist. A swirl of activity surrounded the ship. Workers carried boxes to and fro. Native Americans paddled by in their bark canoes. Travelers were coming and going: businessmen, ranchers, rough-looking miners, and families too.

The noise and tumult were always thrilling. In her mind, Kate could hear it all. The low thrumming of the steam engine. The slap of the water as it struck the dock. The captain shouting orders. The neighing of horses. Passengers calling hello or good-bye.

By imagining, Kate left her sickroom behind. She traveled on the steamboat through the wild, open lands up the river. She rode with Indian children on horseback across the hills. She felt the thrill of miners who found sparkling gold. She lived the lonely life of ranchers on the endless plains.

Kate thought of all the people who had traveled up and

down the Missouri River. She thought of the Indians and the explorers she learned about. She thought of the pioneers whose wagon trains followed the river shore.

Most of all, she thought of all the African Americans who had traveled up the Missouri, seeking a better life on the frontier. Her own family was among them.

Kate's thoughts were interrupted by the sound of footsteps. Her mother came into the room.

"Is it time for my studies?" Kate asked. She was so ill that she couldn't go to school. Her mother, who had been a teacher, gave her lessons at home.

"Not now, dear," Mrs. Chapman said. "We have a visitor. Do you feel well enough to join us?"

"Oh yes!" answered Kate happily. Books and conversation were her only entertainment. With visitors came new stories of the world beyond her door.

Wrapped in a warm blanket, Kate curled up on her mother's lap. She peeked at their visitor, thinking how she would describe him in a story. His skin is the color of coffee, she thought. His eyes sparkle like the river in the sun. He has a deep and comforting voice, like the sound of the river flowing.

His voice filled the room now, as he spoke. "I have traveled across the whole Dakota Territory," he said. "What I have seen is very encouraging for our race. There are colored miners in the gold fields. Some of them struck it rich! Others have started businesses in the mining towns. Buffalo soldiers are protecting the pioneer communities. Former slaves own

Pioneer woman on the northern plains.

homes and farms and ranches. Our people are succeeding here on the frontier!"

"It's true," Kate's father agreed. "The West is a land of opportunity."

Mrs. Chapman added, "I remember how stories such as yours gave us the courage to move here, to Dakota Territory. Keep on sharing your stories with our people as you travel."

"I will," the visitor answered.

And so will I, thought Kate. That's a promise.

Kate clung to that promise as she struggled with yet another childhood illness. This time, she almost gave up

Sioux camp in South Dakota.

hope. The doctor thought she might die. But Kate fought to stay alive.

When she recovered, she wrote her first poem. She was thirteen years old. She returned to school and continued to write. Soon, her writings were appearing in papers around the country. By age twenty, she was well known.

An excellent student, Kate went on to college. She finally was able to travel as she had dreamed. She finally was able to tell her stories.

She wrote about life in Dakota Territory. She wrote about the achievements of her race. She wished always to inspire other African American children to follow their own dreams.

She wrote:

> Let but our people once unite
> Stand firmly as a race,
> Prejudice, error, strong to fight
> Each here in his place...
>
> Liberty, truly, ours will be,
> And error pass away;
> And then no longer shall we see
> Injustice hold her sway.

# Sarah Winnemucca

*Born: 1844 • Died: 1891*

The growth of western communities brought many changes. For Native Americans, these changes were often painful. With the newcomers came wars and deadly diseases. More than half the Native people of the Old West died.

**Sarah Winnemucca**, a Paiute Indian woman, was a leader in the fight for Native rights. She was one of many women who worked to win a better life for the people in the West.

$S$ arah Winnemucca sat quietly in her grandfather's tent. The great chief was old and very ill. This may be the last time we speak together, she thought, and felt sad.

"Shell Flower," he said, calling her by her Paiute name. "Come close." She knelt beside him.

"Life is changing for the Paiute people. Already you have seen these changes. We are no longer the only ones on this

Paiute woman.

land. White people are coming here, more every day.

"You are young, Shell Flower, but you have already learned much about these newcomers. You have lived among them. You speak their language."

It was true. She had accompanied her grandfather and other Paiutes who went to work on a ranch for a while. Later, she lived with a white family who had a daughter her age. She had learned to speak both English and Spanish. She even had an English name now, Sarah.

Grandfather continued. "I want you to make a promise. I want you to study at the white people's schools. You must learn about their ways. You must help our people and theirs to live next to each other in peace."

"I promise, Grandfather," she replied. "I will do as you ask."

Sarah had always obeyed her grandfather's wishes. For as long as she could remember, he had been the Paiute's most respected leader. It was to his tent that people came when they needed advice. It was here that they gathered to discuss important decisions for the tribe.

Many times, Sarah had come to Chief Winnemucca too. He had taught her important lessons: Never make fun of anyone. Treat every person with kindness and respect. There may be much to learn from people who are different from you.

Sarah thought about these lessons as she prepared for her trip. It would be a long journey, for the school lay across the

Traditional Paiute home.

mountains, far to the west.

She was proud that Grandfather had chosen her to help their tribe. But there were many things she would miss. Paiute girls liked to play with dolls and make figurines in clay. Sometimes, they made a model village with tiny lodges and cooking fires made of grass and twigs; sometimes, they made little clay animals and played at hunting.

Each year, in spring, they enjoyed the festival of the flowers. Most Paiute girls were named after the flowers that grew around their camp. At festival time, they gathered the blossoms that shared their names. Each girl made a beautiful wreath of blossoms to wear.

At the boarding school, there were no Paiute friends or bright fields of flowers. Even worse, there was prejudice. Some of the parents of other students complained. "We won't allow our daughters to go to class with an Indian!" they said. Sarah was sent home.

Even more painful experiences were to come. Sarah was there the first time that whites attacked the Paiute camp. All the food her family had gathered for the winter was burned. More attacks followed. The Paiutes were forced to move again and again.

The worst times came in 1865. That year, a few Paiutes stole some cattle from white settlers. The army attacked the entire tribe, killing many women and children. Sarah's baby brother, her mother, and her sister died.

But Sarah remembered what her grandfather had said, and she chose to work for peace. War comes when people do not understand each other, she said to herself. I will do all I can to bring about that understanding.

Sarah Winnemucca went to the army. "Let me be your interpreter," she said. "I can carry your messages to my tribe and explain my people's response to you." Sarah's offer was accepted.

Her task was often a demanding one. Once, she traveled over one hundred miles, alone, to talk with members of her tribe. No one else dared to make the trip. But Sarah was determined. She mounted a horse and set off into the roughest part of Idaho.

Hour after hour, she pushed on, climbing rocky mountain-sides, descending steep valleys, crossing swift streams. Finally, exhausted, she arrived at her father's camp and delivered her message. With Sarah's help, the Paiutes escaped danger.

Sarah Winnemucca.

But Sarah Winnemucca's hard work and determination could not solve a more difficult problem. The government leaders did not keep their promises. They promised food and supplies that did not come. They promised peace but attacks continued. They promised good land but sent Paiutes to barren desert where no food could be found.

Sarah knew she must try something else. It was time to speak out. She traveled around the country, telling the Paiutes' story and calling for justice.

Sarah Winnemucca became so well known that she was invited to speak with the president of the United States! Sarah went to Washington, D.C. With her father and other Paiute leaders, she met with President Rutherford B. Hayes. She spoke with him and with his director of Indian policy. She spoke convincingly.

Promises were made, but like the others, they were not kept. Sarah Winnemucca must have been disappointed, but she kept working. She divided the rest of her life between speaking and teaching. She started a school for Paiute children. There, she was able to pass on lessons from her grandfather: Treat every person with kindness. Respect those who are different from you. Do what you can to work for peace.

# SELECTED BIBLIOGRAPHY

Alter, Judy. *Women of the Old West*. New York: F. Watts, 1989.*

Armitage, Susan H. *Women and Western History*. Wellesley, Mass.: Wellesley College Center for Research on Women, 1984.

Armitage, Susan, and Elizabeth Jameson. *The Woman's West*. Norman, Okla.: University of Oklahoma Press, 1987.

Bowman, J.N. "Juana Briones de Miranda," *Historical Society of Southern California Quarterly* (Sept. 1957): 227-241.

Brown, Dee Alexander. *The Gentle Tamers: Women of the Old Wild West*. New York: Putnam, 1981.

Gatewood, Willard B., Jr. "Kate D. Chapman Reports on 'The Yankton Colored People,' 1889," *South Dakota History*, (Winter 1976): 28-35.

Gray, Dorothy. *Women of the West*. Oakland, Calif.: Antelope Island, 1982.

Jeffrey, Julie Roy. *Frontier Women: The Trans-Mississippi West*. New York: Hill & Wang, 1979.

Johnson, Dorothy M. *Some Went West*. New York: Dodd Mead, 1965.

Josephy, Alvin. *The Indian Heritage of America* (rev. ed.). Boston: Houghton Mifflin, 1991.

Katz, William Loren. *The Black West*. Seattle: Open Hand, 1973.

Liberty, Margot. *American Indian Intellectuals*. New York: West, 1978.

Luchetti, Cathy Lee. *Women of the West*. Oakland, Calif.: Antelope Island, 1982.

McCunn, Ruthanne Lum. *Chinese American Portraits: Personal Histories, 1828-1988*. San Francisco: Chronicle Books, 1988.

Montgomery, James W. *Liberated Woman: A Life of May Arkwright Hutton*. Spokane, Wash.: Gingko House, 1974.

Mora, Jo. *Californios: The Saga of the Hard-Riding Vaqueros, America's First Cowboys*. Garden City, New York: Doubleday, 1949.

Moynihan, Ruth B., Susan Armitage, and Christiane Fischer Dichamp. *So Much to Be Done: Women Settlers on the Mining and Ranching Frontier*. Lincoln, Neb.: Univ. of Nebraska Press, 1990.

Myres, Sandra L. *Westering Women and the Frontier Experience, 1800–1915*. Albuquerque: Univ. of New Mexico Press, 1982.

Niethammer, Carolyn. *Daughters of the Earth: The Lives and Legends of American Indian Women*. New York: Collier, 1977.

Pelz, Ruth. *Black Heroes of the Wild West*. Seattle: Open Hand, 1990.*

Propst, Nell Brown. *Those Strenuous Dames of the Colorado Prairie*. Boulder, Colo.: Pruett, 1982.

Richey, Elinor. *Eminent Women of the West*. Berkeley, Calif.: Howell-North, 1975.

Ross, Nancy Wilson. *Westward the Women*. San Francisco: North Point, 1985.

Schlissel, Lillian. *Women's Diaries of the Westward Journey*. New York: Schocken, 1992.

Schlissel, Lillian, Vicki L. Ruiz, and Janice Monk, eds. *Western Women: Their Land, Their Lives*. Albuquerque: Univ. of New Mexico Press, 1988.

Sheafer, Silvia A. *Women of the West*. Reading, Mass.: Addison Wesley, 1980.

Steber, Rick. *Women of the West*. Prinesville, Oreg.: Bonanza, 1988.

*The Women*. Time Life Books Series on the American West. Alexandria, Va.: Time Life, 1978.

Western Writers of America. *The Women Who Made the West*. Authors, 1980.

Williams, Brad. *Legendary Women of the West*. New York: D. McKay Co., 1978.*

* Juvenile books.

## ILLUSTRATION CREDITS

p. 2: Photo by Edward S. Curtis, Manuscripts, Special Collections, University Archives, University of Washington Libraries, UW16788.

p.5: Mural of Lewis and Clark and Co. at Celilo Falls, by Frank Schwor, Oregon Historical Society, OrHi 527.

p. 8: Photo by Frank LaRoche, Manuscripts, Special Collections, University Archives, University of Washington Libraries, La Roche 1217.

p. 10: Drawing of Fandango Dancers, Unknown.

p. 11: Photo, San Francisco History Center, San Francisco Public Library, Archives, Plate #407.

p. 15: Photo, Security Pacific National Bank Photograph Collection, Los Angeles Public Library.

p. 17: Photo, Manuscripts, Special Collections, University Archives, University of Washington Libraries, UW4930.

p. 21: Photo, Sisters of Providence Archives, Seattle, Washington.

p. 22: Photo, Sisters of Providence Archives, Seattle, Washington.

p. 23: Photo, Special Collections Division, University of Washington Libraries.

p. 26: Photo, Manuscripts, Special Collections, University Archives, University of Washington Libraries, UW6943.

p. 29: Photo, Manuscripts, Special Collections, University Archives, University of Washington Libraries, UW8122.

p. 30: Photo, Manuscripts, Special Collections, University Archives, University of Washington Libraries, NA906.

p. 33: Photo, Special Collections Division, University of Washington Libraries.

p. 34: Photo, Roslyn Historical Society, Roslyn, Washington.

p. 35: Photo, Barnard-Stockbridge Historical Photograph Collection, #8-X145, University of Idaho Library, Moscow, Idaho.

p. 36: Photo, Manuscripts, Special Collections, University Archives, University of Washington Libraries, A. Curtis 19943.

p. 38: Drawing by Selma Waldman, Seattle, Washington.

p. 40: Photo, Library of Congress, Washington, DC, LC-USZ62-35874.

p. 41: Photo by Edward S. Curtis, Manuscripts, Special Collections, University Archives, University of Washington Libraries, UW15289.

p. 44: Photo, Nevada Historical Society.

p. 46: Drawing by Chenoa Turia Yoshe Egawa.

p. 48: Photo, Nevada Historical Society.

## ABOUT THE AUTHOR

**RUTH PELZ** has a longstanding interest in uncovering the hidden histories of women and working people as well as ethnic and racial groups in our society. She is the writer of many published books, including two titles from Open Hand's CONTRIBUTIONS SERIES: *Women of the Wild West* and *Black Heroes of the Wild West*. She has learned from personal experience that history is meaningful only if we see ourselves as taking part in it. She lives in Seattle, where she is an education planner at the University of Washington's Burke Museum of Natural History and Culture.

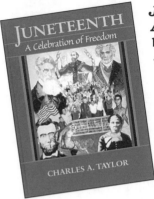

## JUNETEENTH: A CELEBRATION OF FREEDOM
### by Dr. Charles Taylor

Juneteenth, the oldest African American celebration in the United States, demonstrates the jubilation felt on June 19, 1865, when African American people in Texas were the last to be freed from the horrors of slavery, over two months after the end of the Civil War. Dr. Taylor makes information about Juneteenth accessible for readers aged ten and up. Juneteenth is quickly becoming one of the most popular holidays observed by Black Americans; eight states have already made Juneteenth a legal holiday.

32 pages / ISBN: 0-940880-68-7 hard cover / $19.95
with colorful illustrations, archival photographs and historical documents

## HABARI GANI? WHAT'S THE NEWS?: A KWANZAA STORY
### by Sundaira Morninghouse
### with full-color paintings by Jody Kim

December 26 through January 1 will never be the same for seven-year-old Kia and her family. The Edwards are celebrating Kwanzaa, the popular, indigenous, cultural and political observance of the African American experience in the United States. As each day unfolds, Kia experiences the seven principles of Kwanzaa — unity, self-determination, collective work and responsibility, cooperative economics, purpose, creativity, faith — woven into the life of her family and community.

32 pages / ISBN: 0-940880-39-3 hardcover / $16.95 / with full-color original art and a Swahili glossary

## MASTER WEAVER FROM GHANA
### by Gilbert "Bobbo" Ahiagble & Louise Meyer
### with photographs by Nestor Hernandez

Award-winning *Master Weaver from Ghana* provides an enchanting introduction to the art of West African weaving. Kweku, the young son of master weaver Bobbo, learns the value of family, tradition, culture and community ties in the fishing village of Denu, on the Atlantic coast of Ghana. Kweku learns that in life, just as in weaving, "one thread is weak, while threads woven together are strong."

32 pages / ISBN: 0-940880-61-X hardcover / $18.00
with colorful photographs, maps and a glossary

*Children's Book Council's "NOTABLE CHILDREN'S TRADE BOOK IN THE FIELD OF SOCIAL STUDIES 1999"*

**OPEN HAND PUBLISHING, LLC**

**OPEN HAND PUBLISHING, LLC**
*proudly presents the*

# CONTRIBUTIONS SERIES

The CONTRIBUTIONS SERIES, written at a 4th and 5th grade reading level, is also ideal for adult new readers. All books are available in both hardcover and paperback. A curriculum guide is available for each of the five titles.

**SYLVIA STARK: A Pioneer**
by Victoria Scott and Ernest Jones
illustrated by Karen Lewis

**WOMEN OF THE WILD WEST:**
*Biographies from Many Cultures*
by Ruth Pelz

**BLACK HEROES OF THE WILD WEST**
by Ruth Pelz
illustrated by Leandro Della Piana

**PATHBLAZERS:**
*Eight People Who Made a Difference*
by Marilyn K. Fullen
illustrated by Selma Waldman

**GREAT BLACK WRITERS**
by Marilyn K. Fullen

For more information on the
CONTRIBUTIONS SERIES
and the complete list of books
for adults and children from
*OPEN HAND PUBLISHING, LLC,*
please visit our web site:
**www.openhand.com.**